This book belongs to:

Given with
Love by:

Copyright © 2024:Cute-as-a-Bug Books
All Rights reserved

My Very First Valentine's Day!

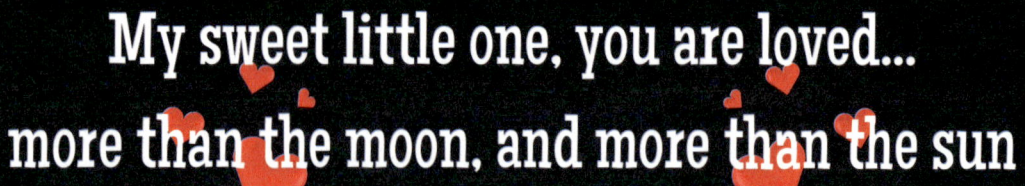

My sweet little one, you are loved...
more than the moon, and more than the sun

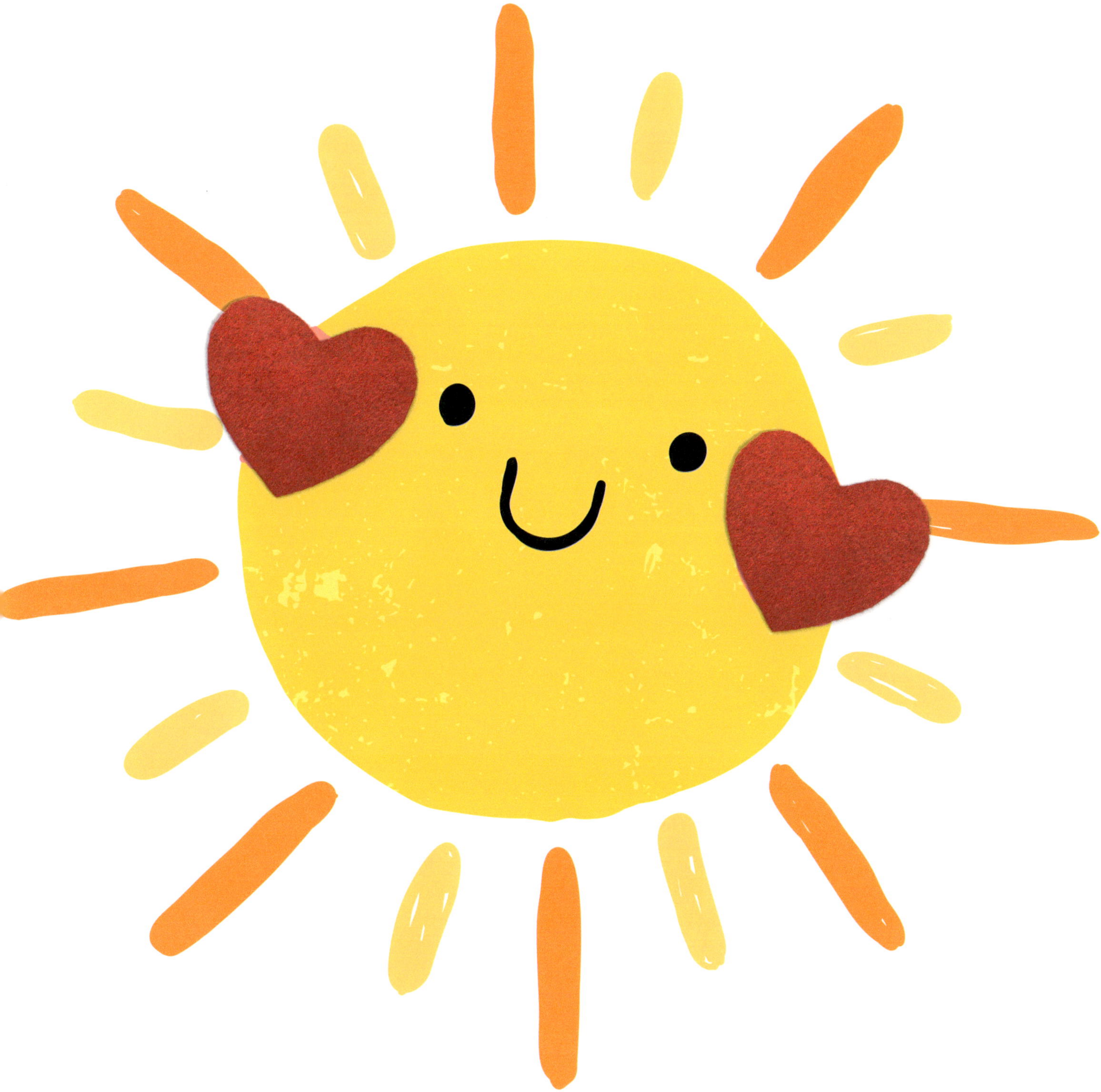

We love you more than all the balloons in the sky, someday you might fly in an airplane, oh so high!

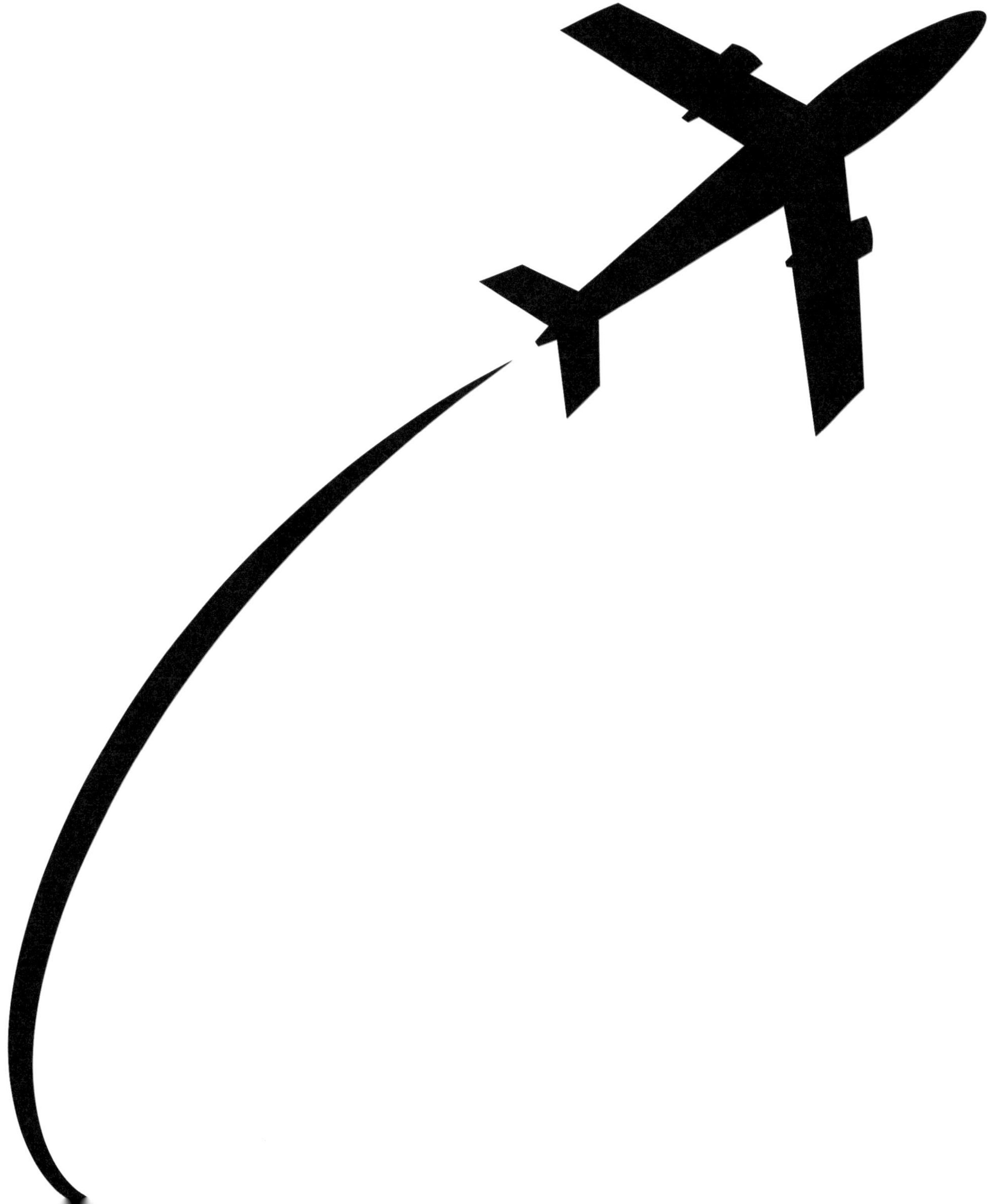

You are cuter than a Songbird, singing a sweet tweet, tweet, tweet!

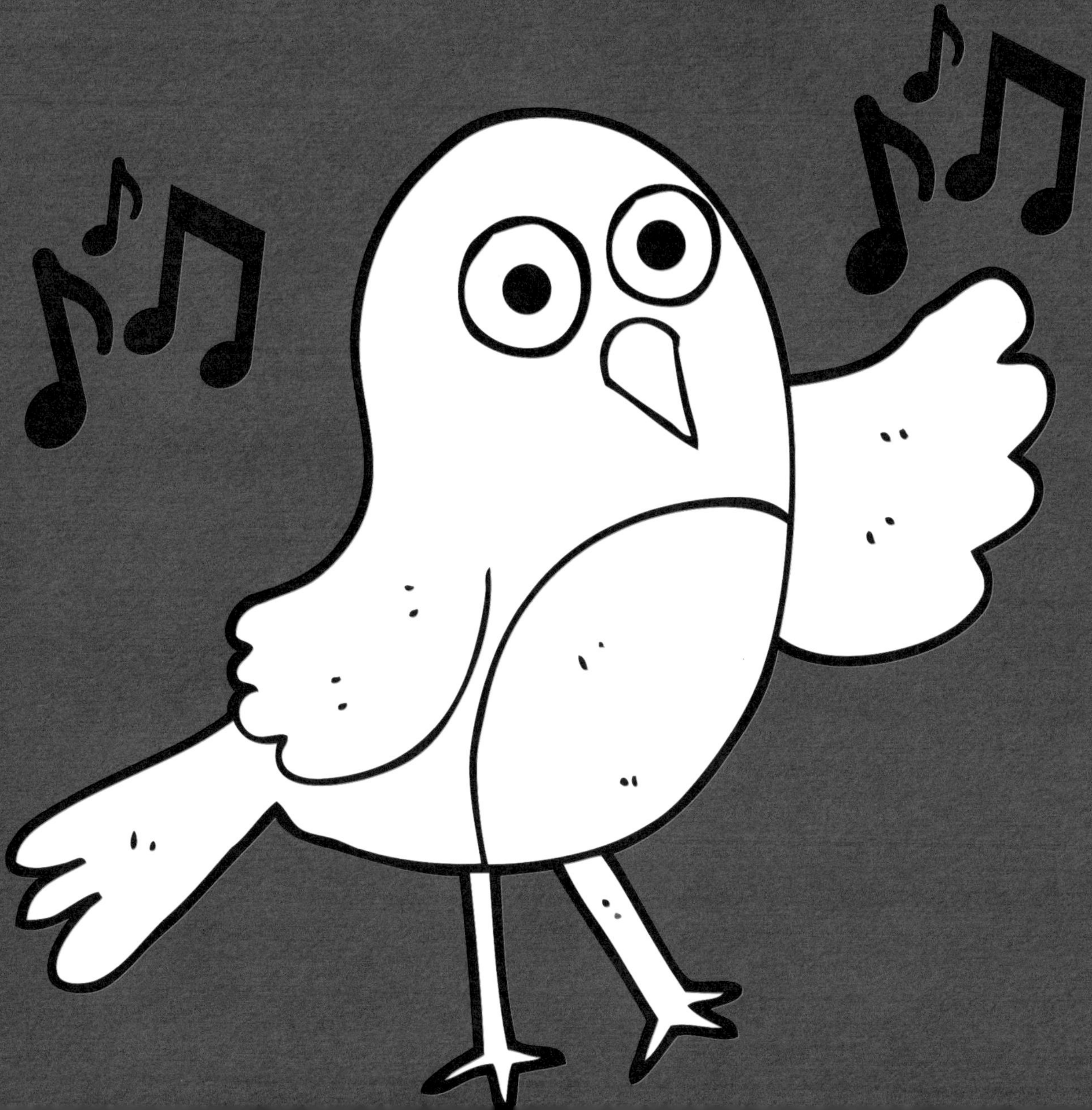

You are sweeter than a dinosaur and their funny dancing feet!

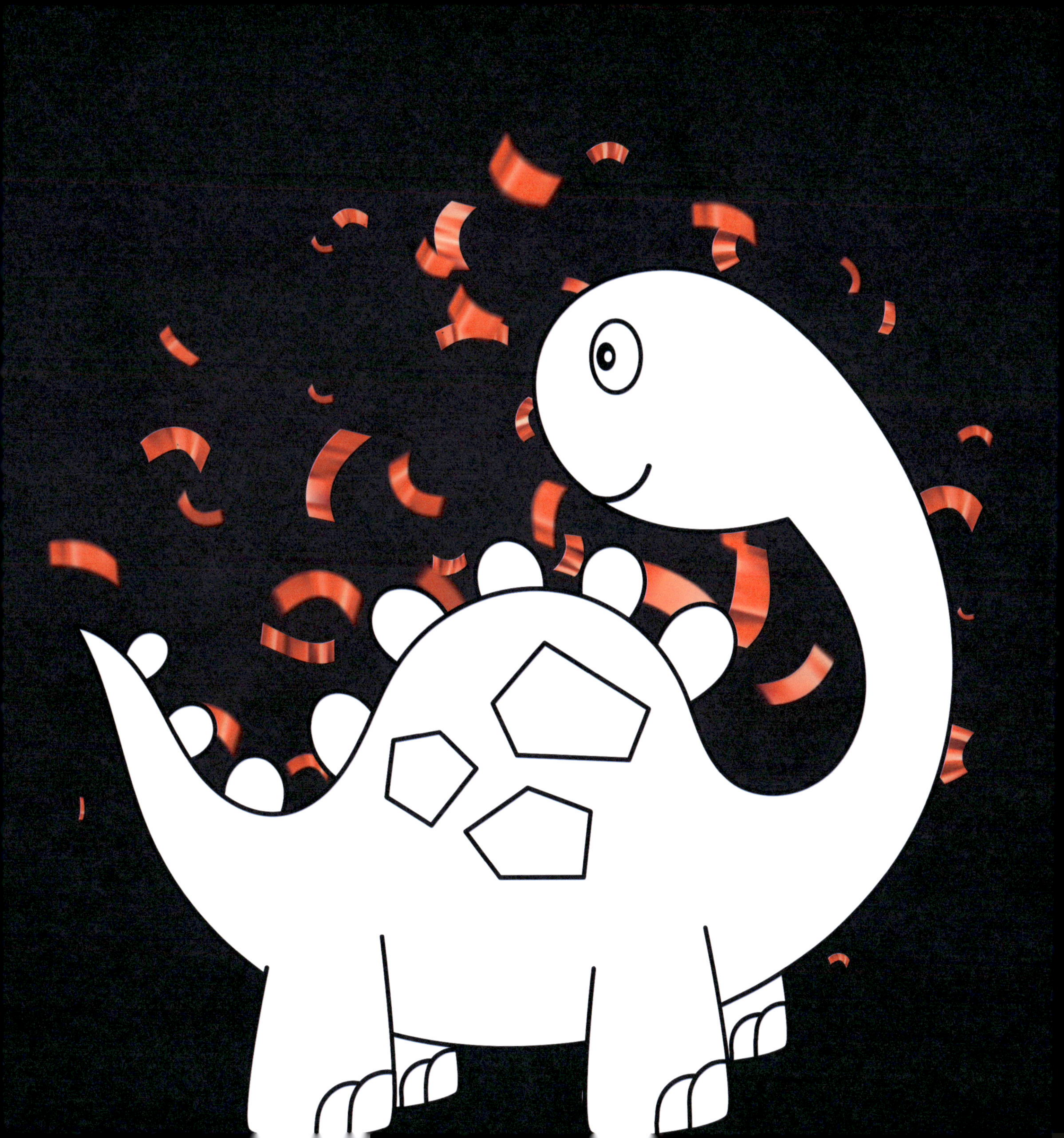

I love you more than a million butterflies, that soar to the sky during a morning sunrise!

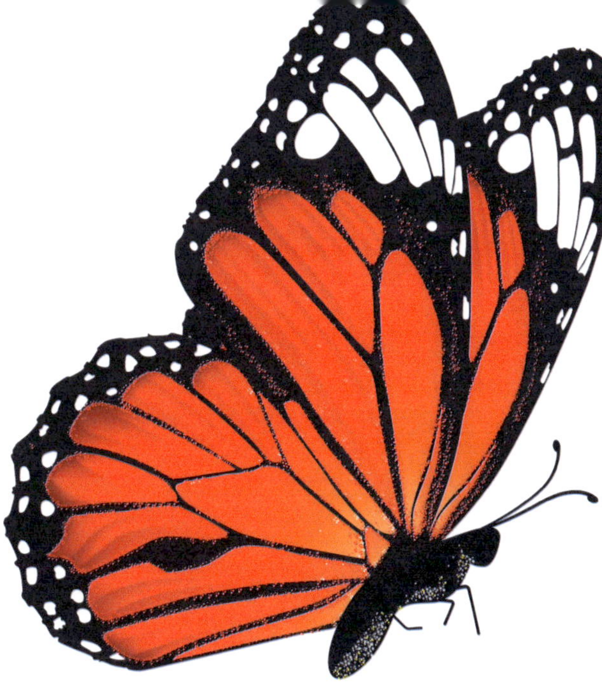
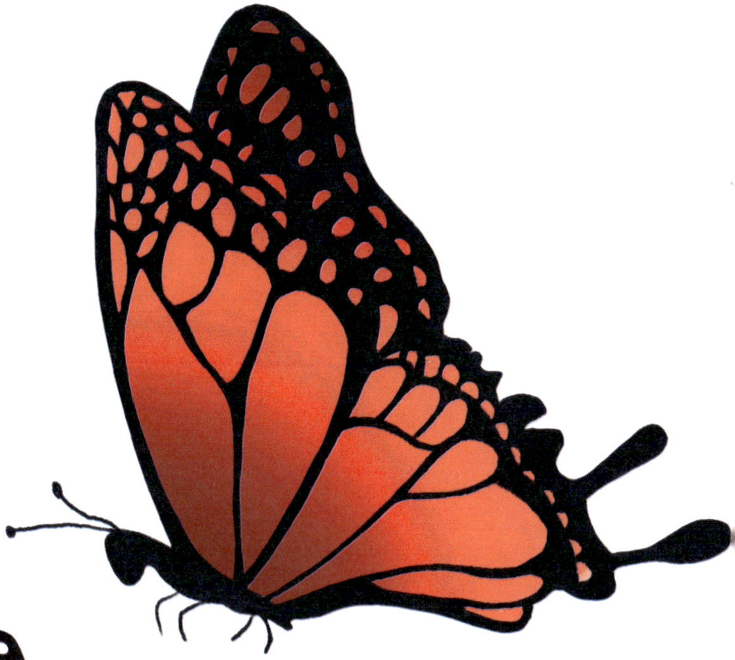
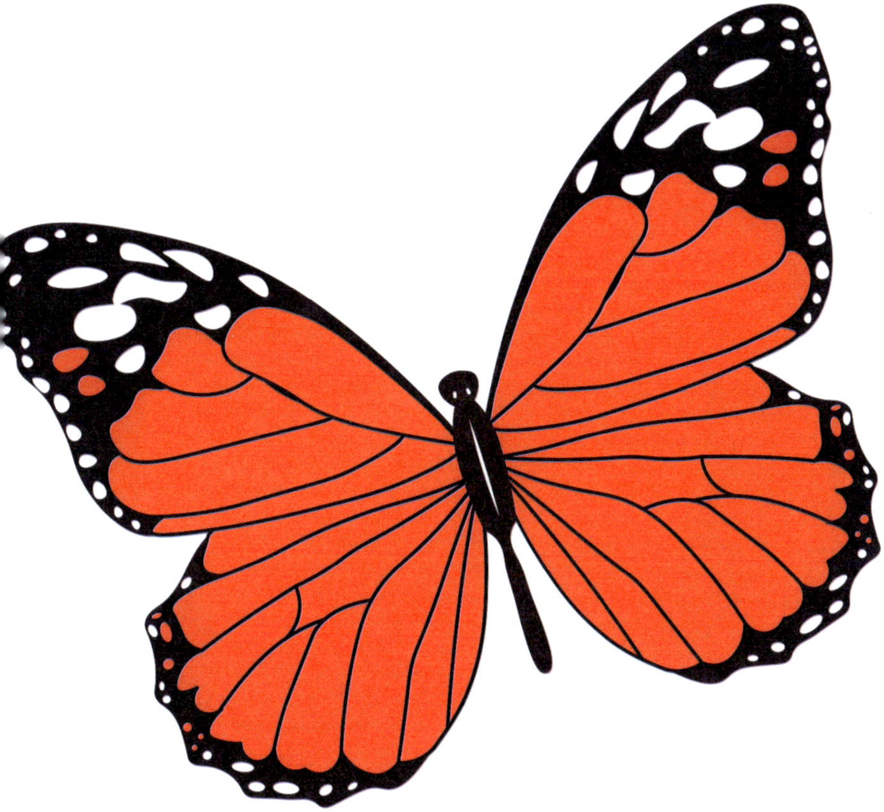

Valentine's Day is special with You!
My love for you will always be true!

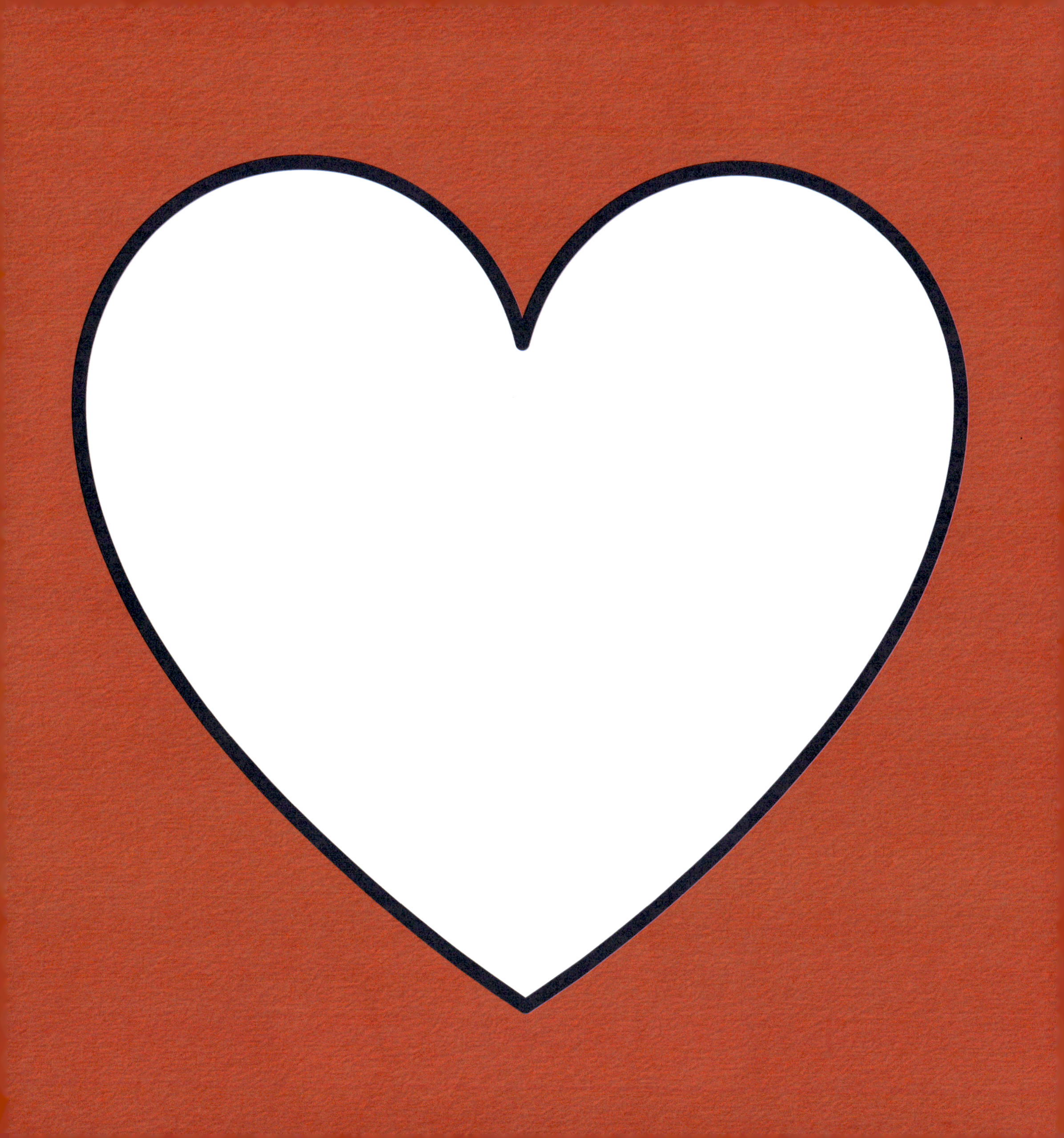

You are special, you are dear!
I'm so glad to have you here!

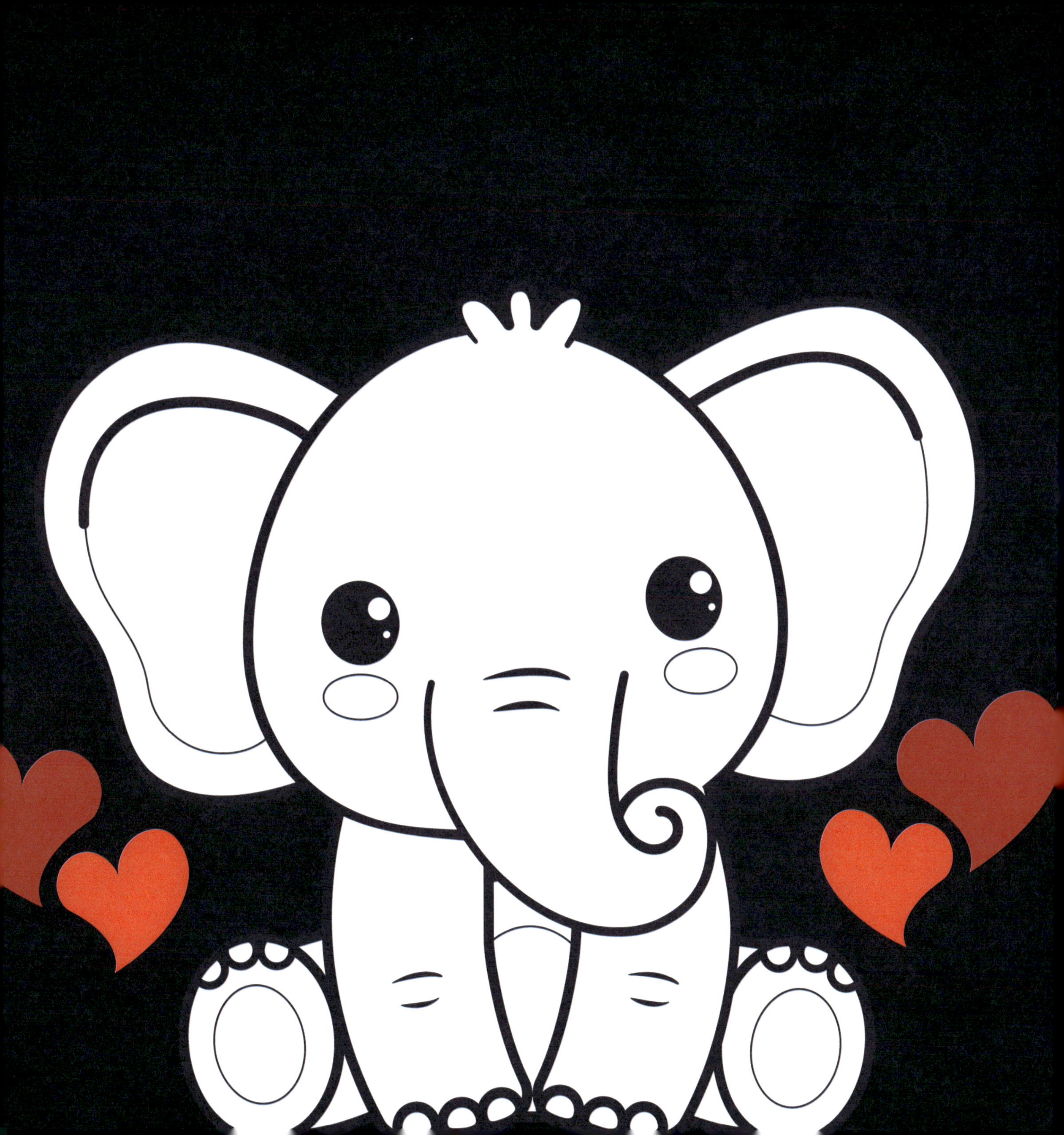

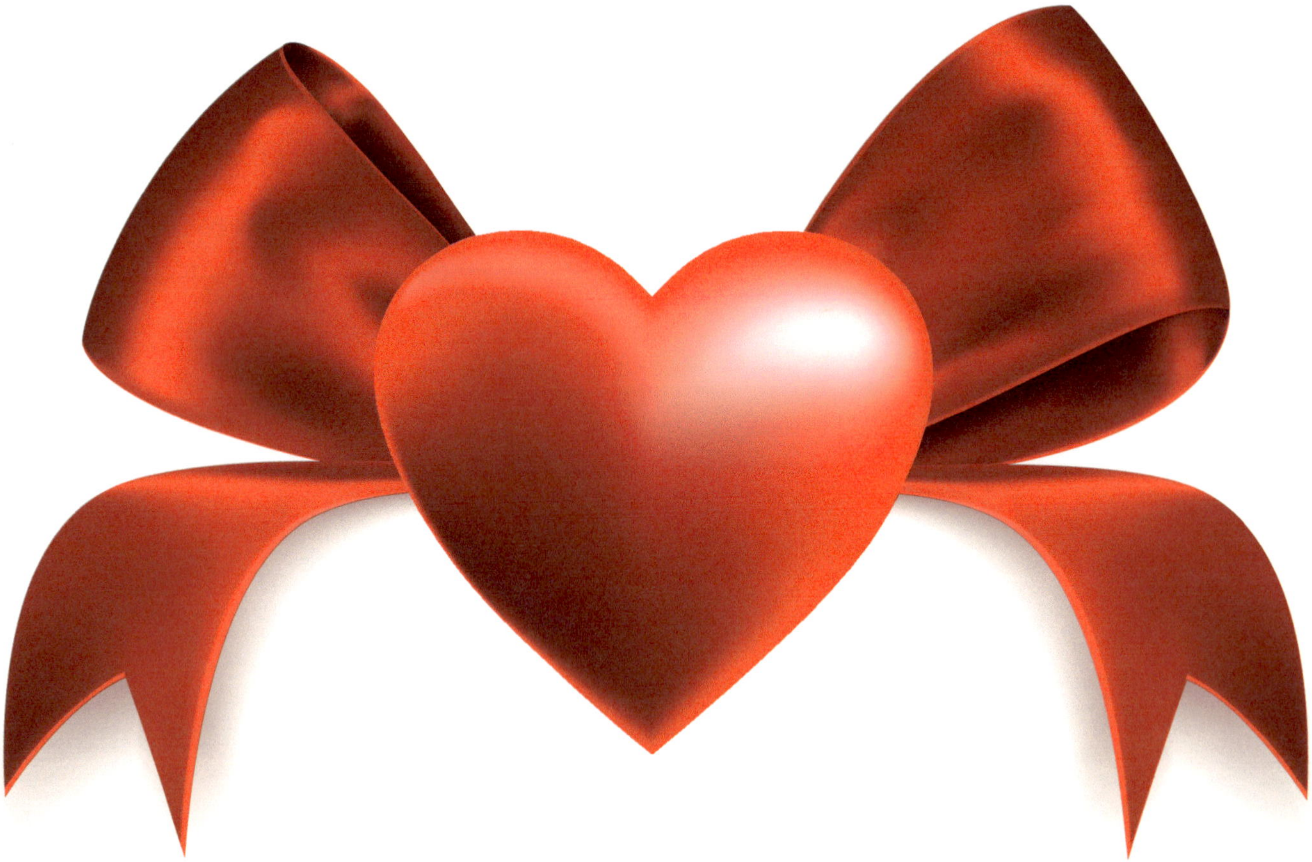

On Valentine's Day, kisses and wishes,
fly through the air, bringing love and joy everywhere!

I'll tell you something special
this Valentine's day!
I love you more than
words could ever say!

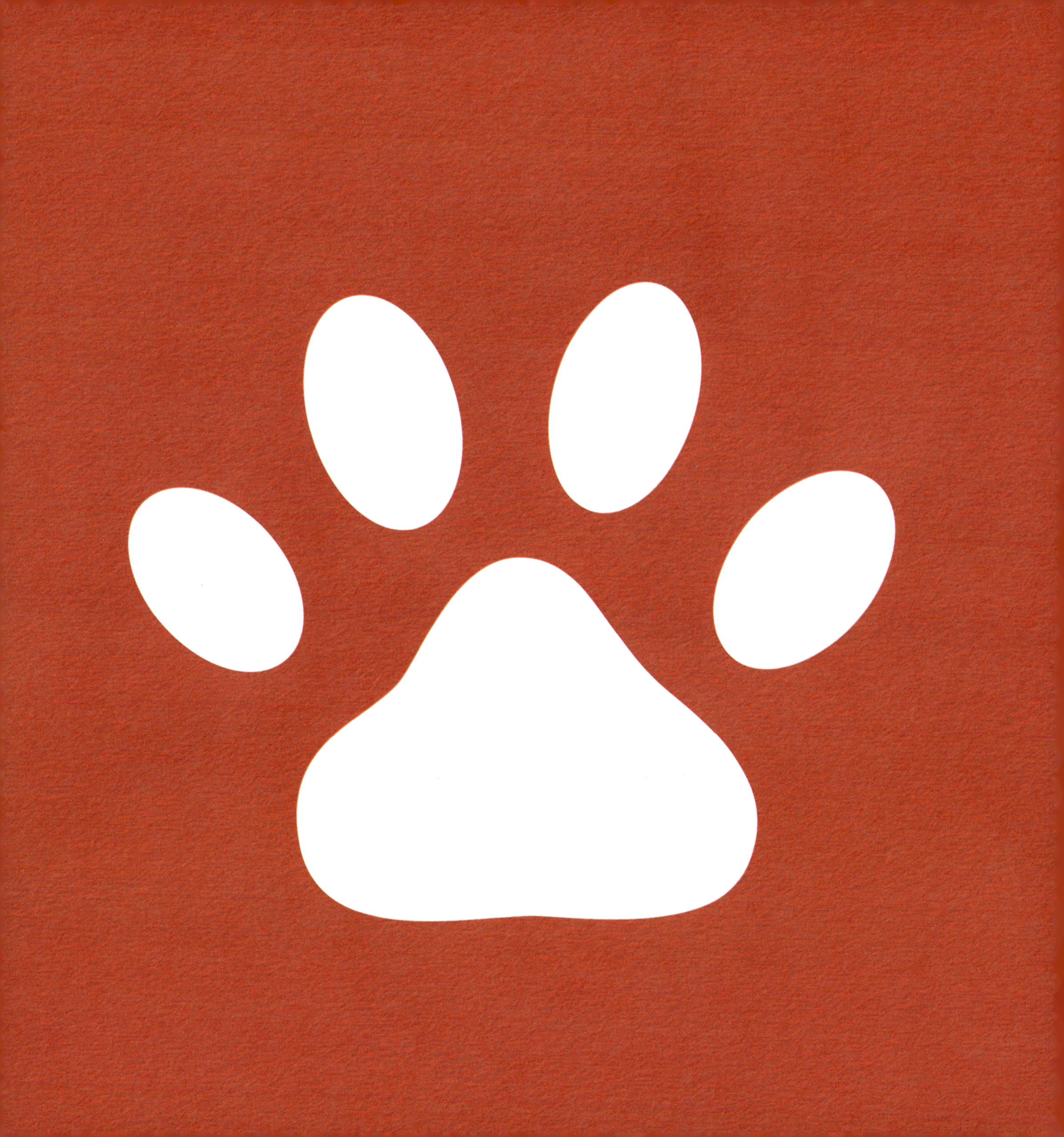

Your cuddles and snuggles are surely the best!

You make our lives beautifully blessed!

Happy Valentine's Day!

The End!

Made in the USA
Columbia, SC
13 February 2025